Succeed @ *Work*

A Workbook for Effective Change

John L. Miller, Ph.D.

FastBreak Press · Thousand Oaks, California

Succeed @ Work
A Workbook for Effective Change

By John L. Miller, Ph.D.

Published by:
FastBreak Press
P.O. Box 7382
Thousand Oaks, CA 91359-7382

Orders@FastBreakPress.com
(805) 492-3400

Unattributed quotations are by John L. Miller.

ISBN: 0-9762923-0-0

First printing 2004

Contents

About the Author

Dr. Miller has made an extensive study of how adults learn to improve their performance at work. His research spans the fields of adult education, psychology, management and leadership.

Dr. Miller is an executive coach who has helped countless CEOs and other senior executives improve their leadership and management performance by using the techniques presented in this workbook. His corporate clients include Fortune 500 companies, educational institutions, non-profit organizations and governmental entities.

In this workbook, Dr. Miller leads you through the steps of change that will help you to rid yourself of the unproductive actions that are hampering your performance and replace them with success-oriented behaviors. By positively changing your behavior, you will gain greater satisfaction from your work, feel more confident in your ability, do a better job and position yourself to advance.

He holds a MBA, a Masters degree in organization development, and a Ph.D. degree in the field of human and organization behavior. He has authored numerous articles, contributed chapters to books, and has been a featured speaker at national seminars and symposiums. He is Associate Professor of Organizational Leadership at Biola University and has also taught the subjects of leadership and organizational behavior at the undergraduate and graduate levels at several other leading universities.

Preface – Note to the Reader

This workbook has been designed to guide you through a process of self-improvement that will result in demonstrable new and more successful behaviors at work. While it is designed to help you deal with immediate performance issues on your job or in your career, it will also teach you the process of successful change that will empower you to grow for the rest of your life.

The workbook is comprised of information on how personal change happens as well as a series of exercises aimed at helping you turn virtually any unwanted behavior into effective performance. The information on change is based on psychological research as well as my personal experience in coaching hundreds of managers and executives to improve their performance at work. The exercises are designed to guide you on your journey by helping you to identify and change the behaviors that are keeping you from getting the most from your job and your career.

This workbook does not offer specific information on how to improve your interpersonal relations, delegate more effectively or get the next promotion. There are other books that will offer you content in these areas and many more. Rather, this workbook addresses the *process* of changing your behavior and improving your performance. That's where most content-oriented books fail. That is, they offer you helpful information but ignore how you are to apply it in a manner that will change your current behavior and bring you success.

The workbook begins with a chapter on the dynamics of personal change and a description of the types of exercises presented in the workbook. Chapters two through seven each deal with a distinct phase of the change process and lead you through the 24 individual steps and related exercises that will help rid yourself of unproductive behavior and develop a new and effective way of acting. The workbook is designed to be comprehensive. You may feel, however, that you do not need to complete each step or all of the suggested exercises. While this is your choice, I would encourage you to read each step and the associated exercises. At the conclusion of your review, if you feel that you have satisfactorily completed the step or any of the exercises, you may skip them. The eighth chapter offers some final thoughts and words of encouragement. Congratulations! You are about to embark on a journey that can change your future at work.

Acknowledgements

This workbook is a product of years of research and practical application in helping people change and become successful at work. However, were it not for the helpful suggestions offered by some of my most valued colleagues who reviewed the workbook, I am sure it would not be as helpful and valuable.

In particular, I would like to thank Dr. Kirk O'Hara of Spherion Human Capital Consulting who provided a comprehensive and detailed review of the workbook. His comments helped bring the book to its final form and content. Dr. O'Hara is an organizational consultant and business coach.

I am especially grateful to Dr. Bruce Heller, an executive coach and psychologist who provided encouragement as I wrote the book. Dr. Heller is an expert on the process of personal change and has provided me with a great deal of insight into the psychological basis of human development.

I would also like to express appreciation to Dr. Brian Underhill a widely-recognized expert in the design and implementation of executive coaching solutions. Dr. Underhill has been a trusted friend, colleague and advisor. He has been instrumental in fostering the refinement of my own coaching philosophy.

Dr. Rex Johnson, an educator, author and psychologist, also provided a great deal of help as I put the finishing touches on the book. Dr. Johnson is Associate Professor at Talbot School of Theology and also teaches in the Masters of Arts in Organizational Leadership program at Biola University. He has contributed to many professional journals and texts, and has published several books to include co-authoring *Characteristics of a Caring Home.*

I would also like to thank Timothy Smith, MA. Tim is a family coach in Thousand Oaks, California, and co-founder of Life Skills for American Families. His insight into counseling techniques has honed the rough edges of my own philosophy about self-coaching. Tim is also a noted speaker and author of several books to include *The 7 Cries of Today's Teens.*

Last, but far from least, I would like to thank my wife Joyce and daughter, Andrea Davis, for their countless hours of proofreading and editing. They have been a source of on-going support throughout the writing of this workbook.

$\mathscr{I}$NTRODUCTION

Have you ever tried to go on a diet to lose a few pounds only to find you gained the weight right back? Ever tried to get your desk organized only to find that after a few days it looked as messy as before? Ever tried to change a nagging habit only to wind up back where you started?

If you're like most people, you struggle to make a little progress and then fall back into your old ways. That's because permanently changing troublesome behavior is more difficult than most people realize. Many people erroneously blame themselves and attribute their failure to a lack of willpower or some other character defect. But research on behavior change indicates that making a positive and lasting change in your behavior requires more than willpower and has nothing to do with your character.

> *"The truth is that you can spend your life any way you want, but you can spend it only once."*
>
> John Maxwell

As an executive coach, I see many clients who have failed in their previous attempts to change ineffective behaviors on the job. These unwanted behaviors are standing in their way of immediate job satisfaction and, often, limiting their possibility of landing a desired promotion. Considering that my work is to help people successfully adopt new and more effective behaviors, I have made a study of how people can successfully change their old and unwanted behaviors and replace them with new ones that make these individuals more effective on the job. (I am using the word "behavior" to include overt actions as well as internal feelings.) In short, I help them change to succeed.

During my journey towards understanding the process of personal change, I have explored a variety of topics from brain physiology to psychotherapy. As the result of my research and practical experience, I have adopted a six stage model of behavioral change. I have repeatedly witnessed the model working for my clients and I am confident that it can help you too. By using this model I believe that you will harness the power to successfully change your behavior for the better whether you are interested in gaining new management and leadership skills, improving your appearance, overcoming fears of public speaking, developing greater self-confidence or any one of a number of other behaviors required to be successful at work.

This workbook is designed to help you become successful in mastering your personal change process by giving you information about *how* you can change and a series of exercises that will help ensure your progress. It is a *self-coaching* workbook meaning that it will provide direction as you navigate through your own change process. The exercises described in this workbook are the same as those that I have used successfully with my clients. This workbook is designed to be practical and useful. Success, however, is dependent on your hard work and commitment. The exercises serve only as your guide. As you look through the workbook you may feel overwhelmed with the number of steps and exercises presented. Don't lose heart. Take one step at a time.

"*In* order to succeed, your desire for success should be greater than your fear of failure."

Bill Cosby

The Change Process

Research has indicated that the process of change involves six major phases. To be successful in changing your old behaviors and adopting new and more effective new ones, you must take each phase in order. The phases are:

- *Phase 1 - Identifying what you want to change*

  To begin you will identify and gather important information about the general area in which you want to improve.

- *Phase 2 – Making a genuine commitment to change*

  Your ultimate success is related to your fundamental commitment to change. In this phase you will learn how to develop that commitment.

- *Phase 3 – Determining your goal*

  In phase 3 you will sift the information you have gathered in the first phase with the aim of developing a concrete change goal and itemizing specific success-oriented behaviors that, when demonstrated, will lead you to success on your job.

- *Phase 4 – Preparing to change*

  Here you will learn how to properly prepare yourself to overcome the obstacles that may prevent you from taking successful action.

- *Phase 5 – Taking action*

  In this phase you will be acting out your new and improved behaviors. You will learn helpful and proven techniques that will ensure you are successful.

- *Phase 6 – Maintaining your successful new behavior*

  In this last phase you'll learn how to maintain your improved behavior over the long term.

One problem people have in successfully changing their behavior is that they hastily try to identify the behavior they don't want and then rush head-long into trying to change it. They seldom do a thorough job of working their way through the six phases of successful change. As a result, they fail in their attempts to improve performance. True change is not a hit or miss proposition. It takes planned and focused effort, and discipline to navigate through each phase.

Nature of the Exercises

Before we start I want you to get a journal in which you will write your thoughts, observations, feelings, revelations and the results of the workbook exercises. Journaling is a wonderful way to express what you are feeling as you progress through your self-coaching program. As you journal, you will bring forth disassociated ideas, insights and experiences that are "floating" in your brain. Writing them down serves to make them explicit and helps you clearly understand their meaning. Simply thinking about things or even talking about them does not confer the same benefits as writing. To journal, I suggest you purchase an inexpensive spiral notebook, although any kind of notebook (i.e., three ringed, leather bound, etc.) will do fine. For your convenience, I have included a few blank pages at the end of each chapter which you can use as your journal. I am going to ask that you do not share what you have written in your journal with anyone - not even your best friend or your spouse. I want you to be free to write what you think and feel without having to explain it to anyone else.

In this workbook I will present the six major stages of change as well as associated exercises that will lead you on your journey. There are a total of 24 individual steps to successful change. The workbook leads you through each step and offers one or more exercises for each step that will help you apply the step to your situation at work. The exercises have been expressly crafted to make use of some powerful research on how your brain works.

Your brain is a marvel which can store and process information many times quicker than the fastest computer. Your brain is also the seat of your actions and feelings. Recent research in neuropsychology indicates that your behavior becomes programmed into your thinking patterns. As such, much of your behavior happens automatically. That's why you often do the very thing that you want to change. It's programmed into your thinking! In effect, the connections between your brain cells are relatively fixed and cause you to act in a certain and predictable manner. When you learn something you chart a new course between these connections. In a matter of speaking, breaking the cycle of your old behavior becomes a matter of reprogramming your brain's circuits. Fortunately, your brain can accommodate this reprogramming.

The exercises in this workbook are designed to reprogram your thinking and acting in such a way that you will demonstrate success-oriented behaviors at work. To accomplish this, the exercises make use of both your cognitive and emotional powers. Getting in touch with these powers and leveraging them towards a positive change in behavior can help change how you think and act. Given the importance of the exercises, I want to explain below the various kinds of exercises that are used in this workbook and why they are useful to you.

- **Writing exercises**

> *"Learning to write is learning to think. You don't know anything clearly unless you can state it in writing."*
>
> S.I. Hayakawa

The reason that I want you to keep a journal and write down your thoughts is because the mere act of writing activates the parts of your brain which help you synthesize and memorize the information you write. Physiologically, the activation of a certain portion of your brain results in increased blood flow and metabolism to that area. Writing, therefore, helps focus the power of your brain and reinforces the learning you will be experiencing in each exercise. It is important to reinforce your thoughts and learnings by reviewing the writings in your journal on a regular basis.

- **Information-gathering exercises**

Gathering information helps you gain a broader intellectual understanding of the behavior that you want to change. Information forms a basis for understanding. With information you can engage the "thinking" circuits of your brain. Intellectual understanding is an important tool in helping you change. The greater the understanding about the behavior you want to change, the more intelligent assessment you can make about exactly what you need to change.

- **Evaluative exercises**

  Some exercises ask you to evaluate and weigh certain information or develop a list of pros and cons. These kinds of exercises also activate the thinking portion of your brain which allows you to process information in a helpful, logical and thoughtful way. Evaluative exercises help you see more clearly the need for change. Studies have shown that the more you value the benefits of change, the greater is the possibility that you will invest the time and effort needed to successfully change.

- **Visualization exercises**

  Professional athletes use visualization exercises to mentally picture themselves running a race, jumping over a high bar, catching a pass or shooting a basket. Their visual memories chart a course in their minds that help their body and brain work together during competition. In a similar manner, I use visualization exercises frequently with my clients. Visualizations are thoughts or mental images that you create. They have actual physical properties and your body reacts to them. Visualizing creates new pathways in the brain that enable you to see yourself successfully acting out your desired behavior. As you visualize successfully acting in a new way, you create a positive memory. Then, when you are ready to actually demonstrate your new behavior, your brain returns to the memory of your visualization which provides a pathway to successful performance. Interestingly, the brain has a hard time distinguishing between actual behavior and that which you visualize. Therefore, from the brain's standpoint, visualizing a new behavior is just about as good as actually doing it. The more you visualize yourself as being successful, the more successful you will become.

- **Feeling-appreciation exercises**

  In addition to visualizing an experience, some exercises ask you to appreciate how you feel when you take a positive action or visualize yourself successfully performing a new behavior. Your brain stores these feelings as positive memories. As you draw upon these memories (including the ones that you visualized), the brain connects them and melds them into a powerful force that you can use to change your behavior.

Feeling appreciation exercises, therefore, can be used as a strategic lever to encourage and emotionally support the process of change.

- **Self-image exercises**

> *"The problem is not so much in developing new ideas as in escaping from the old ones."*
>
> John Maynard Keyes

These exercises are specifically designed to help you see yourself as a competent person who is fully capable of changing your behavior. Psychological studies have indicated that how you see yourself is critical to how you act. It is natural to be faced with self doubt about your ability to change a long standing and troublesome behavior. However, to be successful at changing an unwanted behavior you must feel confident that you can change. You must begin to see yourself in a positive manner that nurtures your feelings of competence and personal mastery. To accomplish this you may need to reprogram yourself by adding to the reservoir of positive memories that feed your sense of self-confidence. There are a variety of exercises in this workbook designed to help you create a new positive sense of self.

- **Emotional-energy exercises**

A few of the exercises ask you to engage your emotions as a way to help you energize to change. I have found that many of my clients think of change only as a cognitive process. That is to say, they believe that all they must do is intellectually understand their problem and then use their willpower to drive the new behavior they want. The truth is that emotional energy is more important in the process of change than is intellectual understanding or sheer will. Your emotional energy acts as an electrical charge and activates certain chemicals in your brain that cause helpful changes in your body (elevated blood pressure, increased respiration, etc.) that support change.

- **Self-awareness exercises**

  Unfortunately, one consequence to our fast-paced society is that you may not spend sufficient time appreciating your own thoughts and feelings. If you don't know how you are feeling about a situation, you are just reacting to life's challenges and have lost touch with the richness and texture of your own feelings. Some of the exercises in this workbook ask you to get in contact with yourself and identify how you are feeling at any given point in time. It is important that you frequently practice these exercises. Take the time to "read yourself" and see what's going on inside. It's hard to make changes on the outside (i.e., your behavior) if you don't understand how you are feeling on the inside. Remember that the inside governs the outside.

- **Helper exercises**

  Many people feel embarrassed when they have a "problem behavior." They try to cover it up. After all, no one likes to admit that he or she is not perfect. However, experience shows that the people with whom you come in contact are aware (if not more aware) of the very behavior that you want to change. In fact, others can often see your unwanted behavior in more objective and unvarnished ways. Research shows that other people can play a major role in helping you successfully change your unwanted behavior. For example, others can give you feedback about how they see you acting. Since we are all limited by our own perspectives, this may be important information that has not been fully considered previously. In addition, others can offer support, insight and caring to help you over the rough spots in the change process. Some of the exercises in this workbook will have you engage this powerful support network to help you reach your goals.

- **Decision exercises**

    At the end of the second phase I will ask you to make a formal commitment to change before you move on to Phase 3. Your commitment to change is critical to your eventual success. If you are not committed, you will likely fail in your attempt to change.

" Change your thoughts
and you change
your world."

Norman Vincent Peale

A Simple Model of Behavior

Before we begin, it is important to understand some fundamentals about behavior. Behavior doesn't just happen in a random fashion. In fact, if you can understand what drives your behavior you'll find that it is rather predictable and has been carefully honed through years of practice. Most behaviors in a business context are relatively complex because many dynamic and often conflicting forces (ego, self-esteem, competence, social interactions, security, etc.) are operating. It is important that you understand how your behavior (particularly the behavior that you don't want) is motivated and directed towards satisfying a need.

One simple model that I have found useful in helping my clients understand their behavior is called the "ABCs of Behavior". "A" stands for *antecedent* which is the situation that is stimulating and motivating behavior. "B" stands for the *overt behavior* itself. "C" stands for the *consequence* of the behavior. Consequences bring rewards of some sort. Diagrammatically, it looks like this:

Antecedent   *Behavior*   *Consequence*

The ABCs of Behavior Model

I have found that while my client's behavior is observable, the antecedents of that behavior may require some detective work to identify. For example, some of my clients may complain that they "fly off the handle" at their boss or co-workers without any apparent cause. They begin to make progress when they understand that by blowing off steam they are rewarding themselves through the release of built up tensions. Once they understand how the model works they can often see the factors that are motivating a wide variety of troublesome behavior.

I suggest that you also carefully consider what causes the behavior that you want to change and understand the consequences (rewards) you are receiving from that behavior. (Believe me, if you weren't getting a reward of some kind, you wouldn't be doing it.) Several of the exercises contained in this workbook will help you to understand the causes of the behavior that you are trying to change. As a warning, however, while the antecedents of your behavior may be difficult to identify, the rewards for your behavior may be even more obscure. Even maladaptive behavior has some sort of positive consequences (revenge, etc.). Understanding how you reward yourself for your unwanted behavior is critical in attempting to replace your existing rewards with new ones that are more effective in producing the success-oriented behavior that you want.

Let's take an example to illustrate how difficult it is to truly understand the causes of behavior. Mary, one of my clients, had a very difficult time speaking before a large group. Her fear was holding her back at work. Mary's level of anxiety was so high that she couldn't sleep at night and her nerves were on edge for days before a speaking event. She would agonize over the mere thought of standing before a large group of people. Mary's mind was flooded with negative thoughts which convinced her that she would fail. She reported that she did a "terrible job" when she finally delivered the presentation. She was nervous, her voice trembled, she easily lost her place and quickly got flustered in front of a group. Try as she might, Mary always seemed to fail. After a few coaching sessions she disclosed that she was constantly criticized by her parents. As we talked, it became more apparent that Mary felt the need to fail in front a group to prove that she "really wasn't any good, just like her parents said." This rationale may sound like convoluted thinking. After all, why would a person intentionally try to fail? In this case, Mary's failing reinforced (rewarded) her own internal self concept that she was a failure. She, in effect, was punishing herself just like her parents had done. She was living out a script that her parents had written for her. The point is that all of our behavior is motivated by a need. Sometimes the need is expressed through behavior in a healthy fashion and sometimes, as in Mary's case, it is not. Using the simple model of behavior helped Mary better understand the ABCs of her maladaptive behavior. Once Mary understood what factors were motivating and rewarding her behavior we were able to work on exercises designed to build her self-esteem and shape a more successful self-image. Like Mary, once you understand what motivates your troublesome behavior, you stand a better chance of ridding yourself of the behavior you don't want.

You CAN Do It!

People *do* change their behavior in dramatic ways. Remember the once poor student who made the honor role? The overweight person who became and remained thin? The timid person who developed a remarkable sense of confidence? In fact, the real issue is not *whether* you can change, but rather *how* you can be successful at change. As discussed earlier, recent research on behavioral change indicates that people who are successful at change go through a series of six discrete phases. Each phase prepares the individual for the next. Now, let's get going on your own journey towards successful performance.

"*Human* beings, by changing the inner attitudes of their minds, can change the outer aspects of their lives."

William James

Notes

Notes

Notes

Notes

CHAPTER 2

PHASE 1 - *IDENTIFYING WHAT YOU WANT TO CHANGE*

Tom was a new supervisor in the accounts payable department of a major corporation. This was a good job with a competitive salary and generous benefits. Tom was quiet and shy by nature. He was, however, a hard worker who filled every possible minute on his calendar with a host of work-related activities. He worked well into the evenings just to get his work done. In spite of Tom's hard work, he had inklings that not all was well. For example, Tom would overhear comments from his staff who criticized Tom's ability to supervise. His peers seem to shun him in the cafeteria and Tom felt they were talking behind his back. Tom would go home at night and incessantly worry about his job although he never took any positive steps to investigate or correct the problem. Over time Tom became isolated from his co-workers and staff. Eventually, Tom became so overwhelmed and depressed with hidden fears that he quit. His action startled his boss, co-workers and staff. After all, he had never let anyone else know of his dilemma and never sought input from others.

I met with Tom some time later when he was having a similar problem in his new organization. Tom is an example of someone who did not spend the time to investigate his problem. Like many people who face difficult problems at work, he chose to withdraw. Rather than take proactive steps that could lead to success, Tom chose to take a passive road that led to failure. Tom did not use his natural problem solving abilities to define the exact nature of the problem. The lesson we learn from Tom's behavior is that we really can't escape our problems. Rather we need to confront and deal with them before they take control of our lives. Here's how you do it.

Step 1. Gather Data

We all have some idea of things that we can do better. Often these ideas are "fuzzy" and sometimes inaccurate. As you begin an effective change process you need to clearly and accurately identify the areas that really need to change. While your intuition about these areas may be correct, it may also be wrong..

Potentially, you have at your disposal at least four ways of gathering data about your performance.

- Your organization, for example, may have a formal 360 feedback survey available. These surveys ask the people around you (i.e., your boss, peers, direct reports and customers) to help identify your strengths as well as areas where improvement is necessary. These surveys are often computer generated and provide extensive amounts of data from the people with whom you work.

- Your previous performance reviews are another important source of data and give you clues as to how your boss perceives the areas in which you can improve.

- You can also interview some colleagues with whom you work closely and ask them to give you candid feedback about your performance.

- Lastly, you may already have some idea of important areas in which your performance can be improved. Your personal insight may come as a simple "gut feeling," your sensing of your own performance, or from comments voiced by others.

Each method of gathering data can offer unique perspectives. Ideally you will have available all four ways of gathering information. If not, I suggest that you use at least two. Here are a series of exercises that will help you.

Exercise 1a: Ask your employer for a 360 feedback survey

Ask your Human Resources department if they have a 360 degree process available in which you can participate. While most formal 360 feedback surveys have standard questions, the people who respond to the survey usually have a place in which they can write personal comments. In this way, the survey is "customized" for each employee who is requesting feedback. After you review the data, then record in your journal the phrases or key words (i.e., interpersonal relationships, management skills, etc.) that describe the general areas of improvement identified by each source (boss, peers, etc) who participated in the survey. In addition to the general areas of improvement, record any specific negative behaviors mentioned by your raters which are associated with each area.

> *"The beginning of knowledge is the discovery of something that we do not understand."*
>
> Frank Herbert

Exercise 1b: Review your previous performance reports

It is always a good idea to retain your performance appraisals for several years. While you may not always agree with your boss' comments, his or her insights are an important source of information about how your performance is being perceived within the organization. At a minimum, I suggest that you examine your last two performance reviews. Read them carefully and try to resist becoming defensive. Treat them as an important (but not the only) perception about your performance on the job. After you review the data, record in your journal the pertinent phrases or key words that succinctly describe potential areas of improvement. In addition, record any specific negative behaviors as mentioned by your boss which are associated with each area.

Exercise 1c: Conduct personal interviews
Ask several carefully chosen people with whom you work most closely to meet with you individually and give you feedback about your performance. At a minimum I would suggest that this group include your boss, three peers and three direct reports. Before you undertake this exercise, however, be sure to review the next page entitled "Asking for Feedback." After you review the data from the interviews, record in your journal the pertinent phrases or key words (i.e., interpersonal relationships, management skills, etc.) that describe the general areas of improvement as identified by each source (boss, peers, etc.). In addition to the general areas of improvement, record any specific negative behaviors identified by the people you interviewed which are associated with each area.

Exercise 1d: Do a "Gut Check"
Think about those areas you feel you can improve upon. Write these thoughts in your journal. Once written, review them carefully and ask yourself how real these thoughts may be. If you are unsure, ask people who know you well for confirmation. Record in your journal pertinent phrases or key words that describe what you have identified as the general areas of improvement. In addition, record any specific negative behaviors that you feel you are currently performing which are associated with each area.

ASKING FOR FEEDBACK

I choose to look at honest and caring feedback as a gift. It is someone's perception of your performance. As such, it has merit and is worth consideration. Asking for feedback is sometimes uncomfortable. Here are a few tips that will make it easier:

- Tell the other person that you are going through a self-improvement program and that you would like to get their impression of your performance. Assure them that you will consider the feedback as helpful and constructive.

- Explain to the other person that you appreciate the fact that they might be reluctant to offer constructive feedback, but that you will consider their honesty as a "gift of friendship." Ask them if they have any concerns about sharing their observations. If so, listen carefully and try to address their concerns.

- Ask them a general and open question such as, "As you have observed my performance, what would say are my greatest strengths? Greatest weaknesses?" You might also ask a question like, "What do you think I can do to improve my effectiveness on my job?"

- Generally, people feel more comfortable giving positive rather than negative feedback. You may have to be tenacious to get honest feedback about your weak areas. Keep probing until you feel that each individual has offered as much helpful feedback as he or she is going to give.

- Use positive non-verbal communication (such as an affirming nod of the head, open body posture, direct eye contact) and active listening to let the person know that you are carefully listening and interested in what he or she has to say, and that you want the person to continue offering information. If you don't understand a comment, ask for clarification such as, "I'm not sure I understand what you said. Would you say it in a different way so I am sure that I fully understand your point?"

- Do not ever try to explain why you did something, or offer a rationale or excuse for your actions. Any explanation on your part will be seen as defensiveness and will serve to shut off open communication.

- At the end of the session, thank them sincerely for their help. Tell them that you will seriously consider their feedback.

Step 2. Define Developmental Areas

The previous exercises are designed to help you gather information about potential areas where further development may be indicated. At the conclusion of these activities you will have amassed information that will help you begin the process of defining meaningful coaching goals and a description of the specific behaviors that you want to change. You may, however, have so much information that you don't know where to start. Your objective should be to sift the information and decide on *one* key developmental area in which you want to focus. By way of definition, a developmental area is a theme that identifies a general aspect of work behavior such as delegation, interpersonal relationships or time management.

Exercise 2a: Define and prioritize developmental areas
Carefully review the findings from each of the exercises above with the objective of identifying general themes that are present from your sources of feedback. For example, you may note that your 360 feedback survey, performance reviews and personal interviews all indicate that you could improve in the areas of building a team and working with peers. Both of these topics could be considered as separate and distinct areas of development. Once you have identified the general themes, then give each a name (i.e., teamwork, developing people, etc.) and write them in your journal. These are your developmental areas. Under each area, appropriately group the comments you have noted previously from your data gathering exercises. As a last step, rank the developmental areas from this master list in their order of importance to *you*. (In case you can't find common themes, make a master list of the potential developmental areas that you feel are the most critical to you.) Note that I did *not* say, in order of importance to your boss, your peer group or your direct reports. While their input may be factored into your decision making, it is more important that you identify the developmental areas that you feel are of the most importance - the ones that you really want to change. Now, note the single developmental area that you feel is the most important. This is the area that you will first work on.

Step 3. Gather More Information on Your Top Area

At this point you may or may not find the need to get more information to develop a broader understanding of your key developmental area. If you already have a great deal of information about the area, you may decide to skip this step. However, while this step is optional, gaining additional information can give you new perspectives on how you can improve.

Exercise 3a: Get additional information about your top developmental area

If you think you have a hard time getting along with your co-workers, then get some books that deal with interpersonal relationships. If you are afraid to give a speech, get some books on public speaking or join Toastmasters. My point is that in order for you to understand your problem behavior, you must acquire knowledge about it. Go to the library or book store and look for information that deals with the subject of the behavior you want to change. Select books carefully. Your objective is to gain an overview, not to become an expert. You may find that inquiring on the Internet is also a good source of information. In addition, you can talk to the people who participated in the 360 survey or your boss who conducted your performance review to clarify cloudy points or ask pertinent follow-up questions. As you gather this additional information, take a moment to write in your journal the points you feel are particularly important.

Finding another person who is an effective performer in your developmental area is another excellent way to gather first-hand information about behaviors that are successful in the workplace.

Exercise 3b: Find a role model(s)

Identify one or more people who are able to perform effectively in your developmental area. Simply observing their behavior can give you a great deal of additional information and insight about how you can emulate new and more effective behaviors. Ideally, you will have the opportunity to talk to the role model(s) and find out more about the productive behavior patterns. Make a list of the role model(s) in your journal; write your observations about the effective behavior and any additional comments from your personal interview.

Step 4. Reflect

It is now time to stop, review and reflect on the information you have gathered. Here's an exercise that will help.

Exercise 4a: Reflect on the information gathered
Review the notes from your journal carefully. Pay particular attention to the specific behaviors that are viewed as problematic. Make notes and comments as you attempt to internalize the information. Don't immediately dismiss any observation or comment. Whether you agree with it or not, it is the perception that another had of your behavior and should be considered. I often encourage my clients to review and reflect on their notes several times over the course of a few days. Don't rush through this step. You must give yourself adequate time for good reflection and internalization of the information.

"*Before* it can be solved, a problem must be clearly defined."

William Feather

Notes

Notes

Notes

Notes

CHAPTER 3

PHASE 2 - *Making A Genuine COMMITMENT TO CHANGE*

Sue was a Vice President of Marketing for a major electronics company. She had risen to being an executive by sheer will and technical skills but often found herself plagued by poor peer relationships. "I don't have time to build relationships with my peers. I'm too busy" was her reply each time her boss suggested that she develop a network of her colleagues. After repeated urging by her boss, Sue begrudgingly agreed that she needed to take some positive action. She talked with a few peers in an attempt to gather more information about how they perceived her. Her boss was delighted. However, after a brief initial attempt to improve her relationships, Sue fell back into her old behavior patterns. Both Sue and her boss wondered what went wrong.

Perhaps you've been in the same situation as Sue. You gathered information about the behavior you wanted to change and made an initial attempt to change; but you still failed. The purpose of this phase in the change process is to help you decide if you want to change. I mean *really* want to change! One of the reasons that people are unsuccessful in their attempts to change is that they take their commitment for granted. As such, their resolve to improve quickly fades at the first sign of resistance.

A true commitment to change is an affirmative decision that you will change your unwanted behavior *no matter what you encounter*. It's not based on whether a new behavior is convenient or comfortable at the moment. A statement such as "I'll try" won't cut it. If this is how you are approaching your opportunity to improve, don't waste your time. That may sound harsh, but psychological studies and practical experience have shown me that nothing less than a *full commitment* to change will produce the results you want. Below are exercises that will help you in deciding whether or not you really want to change.

Step 5. Identify Your ABCs

It is now time to turn your attention to your own ABCs of behavior (see page 16) and uncover some reasons for your current behavior. This will take some time and may be personally uncomfortable as you attempt to uncover some of your own motivations and rewards. I am not suggesting that you enter therapy, although you may feel that psychological help will be of value as you complete your journey. If this is your case, I suggest that you seek outside professional help. At this point, I am asking that you take the information and personal insights you have amassed so far and seriously look inward.

Exercise 5a: Uncover the ABCs of your behavior:
Ask yourself the following questions and write the answers in your journal:

- Under what circumstances does my unwanted behavior happen?

- What seems to motivate it?

- How do I get rewarded when I demonstrate this behavior?

Step 6. Energize for Positive Change

I sometimes find that my clients are overwhelmed by their previously failed attempts to improve. This is understandable because repeatedly failing can create a poor self-image and a lack of confidence. By adopting a defeatist attitude, however, they also sell themselves short and may relegate themselves to a career that is far less than they can achieve. They need to be re-energized before they can positively examine the growth opportunity that is before them.

As discussed earlier, even though intellectual inquiry is helpful in increasing understanding, your emotions are a stronger motivator towards making a positive decision to change. While your emotions may have worked against you in the past (fear of failure, lack of self-confidence, etc.), you can now turn them into a positive force. Physiological studies of brain activity show that by arousing emotions the body responds in positive ways to include increasing brain activity, heart rate and blood pressure. These changes tend to energize you. Properly focused, they can help you make an affirmative and meaningful decision to change. I have included several exercises below that have helped my clients muster the energy to change.

Exercise 6a: Look at others who have the same unwanted behavior
Find another person who has the same or similar unwanted behavior. Observe as they act out this behavior. Now think about how others must perceive you when you act in a similar way. Use this information to "build a case" in your own mind about why your unwanted behavior is negative or self-defeating. Write your thoughts in your journal.

People whom you call upon for help can energize you by offering further encouragement and support to change. They can also add additional insights about the behavior you want to change. As mentioned earlier, enlisting support from others is an essential part of any plan to successfully change your behavior.

Exercise 6b: Identify peer coaches
Identify a small group of helpers ("peer coaches") that you feel will be supportive of your efforts to improve. Usually two or three peer coaches are all that you will need. The value of peer coaches is that they see you performing the behavior that you want to change and are willing to offer helpful feedback. It is important that you tell your peer coaches that you are considering making a change in your behavior and you need their help if you are to be successful. This alerts them to the importance that is being placed on their support and advice. Continue exploring your problem with your peer coaches, remembering not to become defensive or offer excuses for your behavior. If you are feeling unsure about your potential to change, confess your self-doubt to your helpers and ask for their

encouragement. You will need these peer coaches throughout your change process, so choose wisely. Characteristics of a good peer coach include:

- An individual who has the opportunity to observe you performing the behavior that you want to change.

- A person who is willing to be open, candid and unbiased in his or her opinion about your performance.

- A person who cares enough to spend the time and effort to give you feedback.

- Someone who is sensitive enough to know when you need encouragement and moral support.

Exercise 6c: Select a mentor
A mentor fulfills a different role from a peer coach. With a peer coach you are looking for feedback. A mentor, on the other hand, gives you advice. A mentor may or may not actually see you performing the behavior that you want to change. Mentors are valuable because of their experience, wisdom and judgment. Characteristics of a good mentor include:

- An individual that has a wide base of life experiences.

- Someone who is viewed as successful within the organization.

- A person who is willing to candidly share his or her viewpoint and experience.

- Someone who is willing to spend the time with you and will take a personal interest in helping you improve your performance.

Another energizing technique is to examine your current behavior in light of your desired self-image. The primary purpose of the exercise below is to help you take stock of your behavior and how it may be in conflict with your sense of self, personal values or goals. Psychological studies have shown that people tend to reject behavior that conflicts with their self-image. Therefore, if you can identify how you want to behave (your desired self-image) you will be more motivated to discard the unwanted behavior that is in conflict with this image.

Exercise 6d: Compare current behavior with the desired behavior
Divide a page in your journal into two sections. At the top of the section on the left side of the page write the title, "The behavior I don't like." In this section write short descriptions about the troublesome or negative behavior that you are now exhibiting. At the top of the section on the right side of the page write the title, "How I want to act." Then directly across from the descriptions of each unwanted behavior, record the desirable behavior you would like to demonstrate. Compare the two and write your conclusions and feelings in the journal.

It is also helpful if you can visualize how your new behavior will enhance your career, work relationships or self-image.

> "If you can dream it, you can do it."
> Walt Disney

Exercise 6e: Visualize your new behavior
Review your list of desirable behaviors from the exercise above. Now, create a vision in your mind of how good things could be when you are successful in changing your unwanted behavior. Be expansive and consider all the facets of your work life that could improve as a result of making a positive change. For example, perhaps you could

have better interpersonal relationships or enjoy the appreciation of your staff when you master a certain management skill or leadership quality that has been lacking. After you visualize a positive way of behaving, take a moment to appreciate how you are feeling when you demonstrate this behavior. Write in your journal a brief description of what you visualized and how you felt when you "saw" yourself being successful.

Step 7. Weigh the Change

To be sure, not all problems are serious enough to warrant the investment of the time and effort that it takes to change. However, problems that are substantially limiting your effectiveness on the job need to be seriously examined. Research on behavior change indicates that people who strongly believe that change is in their best interest are more likely to sustain the change effort over time. Certainly, it is important to get sufficient information about your unwanted behavior. It is also helpful to understand how positive and rewarding your work life could be if you adopted a more effective behavior. But, these steps are only important if they lead to a genuine commitment to change.

Let me give you an example to consider. A few years ago I worked with Martin, a mid-level accounting manager who desperately wanted to give up drinking alcohol. By the time I first saw him he had already gathered information about the health hazards involved with alcohol consumption. He indicated that he did not like the aggressive behavioral changes that overtook him once he started drinking. The only problem was that drinking after hours was considered as part of the social mores of his company and a great deal of "networking" was done at the bar. If he stopped drinking, he would likely lose important opportunities to informally meet with his business associates and potentially risk a desired promotion. To make matters worse he would probably face the consternation of his "drinking buddies" who would like him to continue his social drinking. In order to change this habit, he had to identify and weigh the cost of making the change. Being a good accountant, he developed a "cost-benefit analysis" dealing with the change he was contemplating. After weighing all the factors, he decided to change. Assessing the cost of this change was critical to giving Martin the fortitude and perseverance required to adopt and steadfastly maintain a new behavior pattern.

Exercise 7a: Determine the price you are willing to pay
Small changes may have few risks and the price is correspondingly low. However, major changes usually involve a higher degree of risk for failure or alienation by loved ones and close business associates. Assessing the price before you make a commitment to change is important. Think carefully about the emotional, physical, financial, and relationship costs to you, your associates, your family and others who are important to you. However, also think of the cost involved in *not* making a positive change for each group. Make a detailed list of both factors and write your thoughts in your journal.

Step 8. Commit to Change

Your moment of truth has arrived! If you have followed all the exercises, by this time you should be in a position to make an informed decision about whether or not you *really* want to change. Make no mistake, lasting change is difficult and you will be expected to work hard if you decide to go forward. You may feel reluctant to make a decision at this point. Don't worry, that's natural. Many people face a great deal of self-doubt at this phase of the process.

There are several common reasons. For example, your fear of failing may be limiting your ability to seriously entertain thoughts of changing your behavior. You may think that you are incapable of doing the things that meaningful and lasting change will require. Your previous failures may be haunting you and whispering negative comments into your subconscious. While it is important that you reasonably and fairly consider if you want to change, it is equally important that you understand the reasons for your hesitations. If you really want to change, it is important that you don't defeat yourself with feelings of self-doubt before you give this process of positive change a fair chance. Remember, you can succeed! Those who don't believe they can change, never will. If you really believe that change is in your best interest, then put your faith in the change process discussed in this workbook that has helped countless people successfully change unwanted behavior.

Exercise 8a: List pros and cons

Develop a simple list of pros and cons dealing with changing your unwanted behavior. Write in your journal what you will gain if you change and then assign a weight to denote the importance of each benefit. This is the "pros" column. (I suggest using a five point scale with five being the most important.) Now make a list of what you'll lose (or risk losing) if you change and assign a weight to each in a similar fashion. This is the "cons" column. Add the numbers in the pros column and then add the numbers in the cons column. You stand a better chance of making a lasting change if the total in the pros column is greater than the total in the cons column. If the total in the "cons" column is higher, repeat the exercise and reconsider the items in each column and the weight you have assigned. After you repeat the exercise, if the total in the "cons" column is still higher then you should reconsider your willingness to make a change. Studies have indicated that you will not make a lasting commitment to change until the reasons *to change* outweigh the reasons *not to change*.

Exercise 8b: Make a commitment

Ask yourself, "Given all I now know, am I ready to commit to the change process?" If so, write in your journal, "I will commit to myself that I will change my behavior regardless of how difficult it may be. I may have setbacks along the way, but I will not allow myself to fail." After you have written this, tell a few close friends and colleagues about your decision to change and ask them to hold you accountable.

Notes

Notes

Notes

Notes

CHAPTER 4

PHASE 3 – $\mathscr{D}$ETERMINING YOUR GOAL

Jennifer desperately wanted to take control of her job. Endless priorities and an avalanche of work had virtually buried Jennifer at her desk. She had compromised her home life and her family complained that they seldom saw her anymore. She discussed the situation with her boss and co-workers. Jennifer finally made a commitment to do something about it. The following day, however, as she walked into her office, she gazed at the mounds of paper work on her desk, the phone ringing off the hook and the stream of employees waiting outside her door. She slumped back in her chair as she realized that she didn't know what to change. She concluded that her job was simply impossible. Eventually, she gave up on her idea to improve and continued in her old and ineffective ways.

Your immediate challenges may not be as overwhelming as those of Jennifer. However, both you and she face the same question: *change to what?* Gathering information and making a commitment is only part of improving your effectiveness at work. In this chapter we will examine the next phase of the change process. Phase 3 involves setting coaching goals and identifying the specific target behaviors that you will need to perform if you are to fully succeed at work.

Step 9. Decide on Your Coaching Goal

Your self-coaching goal forms the basis of the coaching process because it specifies the end result that you want to achieve. Developing goals is natural because people are, by nature, "cybernetic" - they have the need to work towards accomplishing goals. Without them people tend to wander and become frustrated.

True motivation (that is, motivation that comes from within a person) is based on the simple fact that people are motivated to achieve a goal that they feel is *important to them*. The opposite is true as well. That is, people are seldom truly motivated to accomplish a goal that is only important to someone else.

For example, think about one of your greatest accomplishments at work. Did you work so tirelessly because the accomplishment was important for someone else or because it was important to you? If you are being completely candid, you will probably say that accomplishing the goal was meaningful to you. In the same way, successfully changing your behavior requires you to set a goal that *you* feel is important.

When I get to this stage of the change process with my clients, I help them develop a SMART coaching goal (see the facing page for instructions on how to write a SMART goal). Writing your goal in the SMART format will help you develop a goal that is clear and specific, and one in which you can measure your tangible improvement. You may find that within each developmental area you need to set a handful of coaching goals to reach your desired level of overall performance. *However, it is critical that you do not attempt to work on more than one SMART goal at any one time.* The reason for this is that changing requires dedication, practice and focus. Experience indicates that working on more than one SMART goal at a time is too difficult and the probability of success decreases significantly when multiple goals are tackled. Some of my clients, however, develop two, three or more coaching goals at this point but only attempt to work on one at a time. They often find it helpful to have an "inventory" of SMART coaching goals that set a direction for their improvement over an extended period of time.

As a word of warning, writing a good SMART coaching goal may take several attempts. It can be frustrating because you may write and then rewrite the goal statement until it truly reflects what you want to accomplish. Yet, investing time in refining and crafting a good SMART coaching goal is of paramount importance to your eventual success because everything you do from this point forward will revolve around achieving your coaching goal.

> *"The best way to predict your future is to invent it."*
>
> Alan Kay

DEVELOPING "SMART" COACHING GOALS

Writing a SMART goal is a helpful way to set a clear direction for your change process. The characteristics of a SMART coaching goal include:

S = s*pecific and clear*. An effective and descriptive goal can often be written in one sentence. The language should be clear, simple and concise.

M = *Measurable*. The results sought should be measurable. The measurement, however, doesn't have to be totally quantifiable. For example, your goal can also be measured through qualitative means (such as getting verbal feedback from others on performance).

A = *Action oriented*. Use action verbs in your SMART goal statements such as: *achieve, create, develop, demonstrate, implement, improve, maintain, produce* and *will*.

R = *Results focused*. A SMART goal is focused on the end result you are attempting to accomplish.

T = *Timeframe*. This indicates when the goal will be accomplished. Specific target dates ("I will get it done by July 1 of this year) are much better than vague dates *("I'll get it done sometime this year.")*

Some examples of SMART goals are:
"On a consistent basis as measured by informal discussions with all the members of my team, I will demonstrate cooperation, assistance and support for my team members in helping them reach their output goals for the last half of this year."

"I will improve my ability to successfully lead a group problem solving session as measured by 75% of the group's participants giving me an "excellent" rating and no one giving me a grade below "acceptable" as measured on the group's feedback sheets compiled from September 1 to December 31 of this year."

Some of my clients are initially too conservative in defining what they want to achieve. In first writing their goal they tend to "undershoot" the mark because they lack the confidence that they can fully change. While your goal needs to be realistic and achievable, it can also be a "stretch goal" that takes you out of your comfort zone. One way to set such a goal is to ask yourself what end result you would like to achieve assuming that you will not fail in your attempt to change. This is not to say you should be unconcerned about barriers to your success. However, it is to say that you should strive for being the best you can be. That's what personal growth is all about. Now it's time for you to write a SMART coaching goal.

Exercise 9a: Write your SMART coaching goal
From your journal, review the information and specific unproductive behaviors in the most important developmental area. Think specifically about a description of what you would like to accomplish as a goal. Write your initial ideas in your journal using key words or short phrases. Then group together all your thoughts under common and descriptive headings (such as, "developing staff" or "communicating more effectively to my peer group"). Carefully review the groupings you have developed. My guess is that there may be several different groupings and each one could be developed into a different coaching goal. Select from your list the single grouping that is most important to you. Now review your keywords and phrases from this group and write one SMART coaching goal that focuses on your desired end result. Remember, this may take several attempts. Your next job is to challenge your goal statement. Ask yourself if the goal actually reflects the desired result that you want to achieve. Ask yourself if you have been specific enough in your wording and if the time frame is reasonable. Question whether the measurement criterion is relevant and appropriate. Continue challenging your SMART goal statement and refining it until you arrive at a coaching goal that is "just right" for what you ideally want to accomplish.

Step 10. Define Specific Target Behaviors

You are now ready to consider specific and individual target behaviors that, when performed effectively, will result in accomplishing your SMART coaching goal. Think if it this way: a coaching goal describes an end result while target behaviors are actions that, when performed, will lead you to your goal. For example, if your coaching goal deals with improving time management skills, your target behavior statement might read: "I will prioritize my work each day when I first arrive at my desk." Note that this statement reflects a specific behavior that needs to be performed if you are to accomplish your goal.

Some people tend to get target behaviors and activities in their action plan confused. The easiest way to understand the difference is to think of target behaviors as specific behaviors you want to demonstrate while action steps are "how to" approaches that lead to your target behaviors. As discussed later, each target behavior will have its own action plan.

> *"It's not enough to do your best. You must know what to do, then do your best."*
>
> W. Edwards Deming

Usually, for every coaching goal you will have some behaviors that you are already performing well and some that need improvement. For example, if your goal is improving communications with your direct reports, your data gathering may indicate that you already are clear and concise in your oral communication but you could improve your sensitivity to their feelings. *For purposes of specifying target behaviors in these exercises, you need only be concerned about those specific behaviors that you want to improve.* For every coaching goal you will have at least one specific target behavior. Often you will have several. You should craft your target behavior statements with the same diligence that you used in developing your coaching goal. Each target behavior statement should be *positive and descriptive* of the specific behavior you will demonstrate to reach your goal.

For purposes of illustration, let's assume that you have completed a 360 survey and have also concluded a personal interview with your boss, several peers and a few direct reports. Based on the information you have gathered, you discover that you tend to anticipate your boss' comments and jump in with your opinion before he can completely describe his idea. After some reflection you have decided to make communicating effectively with your boss a developmental area. Let us further assume that you are able to successfully apply many communication skills in a dialogue with your boss. However, the feedback indicates that you do not listen to your boss when he is expressing an idea and you are overly intent on voicing your opinion. As such, you have decided to make listening more attentively to your boss as the subject of your coaching goal. You also decide that you can work on two specific target behaviors that will help you reach this SMART goal. First, you believe that you should use active listening skills with your boss. Second, you decide that you will wait until you are sure that your boss has completed his thought before you chime in with your opinion. Both of these specific behaviors, when added together with your other pre-existing communication skills, will help you reach your overall coaching goal of listening more attentively to your boss. As an example, in your journal you may record the following statements:

- **Developmental area:** Effective communication with my boss.

- **SMART Coaching goal**: Effective immediately, I will listen more attentively to my boss and not offer my opinion about his idea until he has completed expressing it as measured at the end of six months by how my boss and 3 of my peers evaluate my performance in this area.

- **Target behavior #1:** I will use active listening skills (your desired target behavior) each time (when) my boss (who) offers an idea.

- **Target behavior #2:** In every discussion (when) with my boss (who), whenever he offers an idea I will withhold my opinion until I am sure that he has completed communicating his idea fully (your desired target behavior).

As you can see from the example above, a target behavior statement may be written in several different ways. You can write it any way that you feel best expresses your desired specific behaviors as long as the elements (i.e., a positive *description* of your desired target behavior, with *whom* it will be demonstrated and *when* it will be demonstrated) are present in each statement.

Exercise 10a: Pinpoint desirable behaviors

Review the information you have accumulated thus far in your journal that relates to the coaching goal you have decided to address. Pay particular attention to the specific negative behaviors that you have identified from the previous exercises. Divide a page lengthwise in your journal into two columns. At the top of the first column write the title, "Unwanted Behaviors." At the top of the second column write the title, "Desirable Behaviors." In the first column, write concise and behaviorally oriented keywords or statements that relate to describing your unwanted behaviors ("I talk when I should be listening", "I withdraw from conflict", etc.). These are the specific counterproductive behaviors that you and others believe create the problem. Now across from each ineffective behavior, write one or more specific desirable behaviors that you can substitute for each unwanted behavior.

Exercise 10b: Write your target behavior statements

Now review your list of desirable behaviors. See if you can narrow the list down by combining the specific behaviors that closely relate to one another or are duplicative. The objective is to have a concise list of impactful target behaviors that relate to your SMART coaching goal. These are the behaviors that, when successfully demonstrated, will rid you of the troublesome behaviors that you are now exhibiting. Carefully review the desirable behavior statements you have crafted and make your first attempt at writing your target behavior statement in your journal. Now, ask yourself if each statement truly reflects the specific behavior that, when performed, will lead you to your goal. Continue challenging and revising a target behavior statement until you arrive at one that is reflective of the positive behavior that you want to demonstrate. You may have a long list of target behaviors that you would like to demonstrate. *However, you should work on a maximum of two target behaviors at one time.* As in the case of your coaching goals, you can inventory additional target behavior statements. Then, once you have mastered the initial target behaviors, you can then begin working on these other behaviors.

"*O*pportunity is missed by most people because it is dressed in overalls and looks like work."

Thomas A. Edison

Notes

Notes

Notes

Notes

CHAPTER 5

PHASE 4 - *PREPARING FOR SUCCESS*

Jack's inability to effectively confront his boss had been weighing on Jack for some time. He felt that his boss was overly critical of his performance. Jack often felt deflated and belittled when he interacted with his boss. Jack had confronted his boss before, but he invariably got overly emotional and bungled the confrontation. Jack had tried to examine the problem. He read books and even consulted a psychologist. He learned more about himself and gained additional insights about his own behavior. Jack's goal was to deal with his boss in a more constructive way and not just lose his temper. He had made up his mind that he would keep his cool the next time he and his boss had a run in. To this end, he had made a list of the specific target behaviors that he wanted to demonstrate. It didn't take long before his boss made another comment that Jack interpreted as demeaning. Jack's blood immediately boiled and he reeled off with a barrage of stored up emotion.

As Jack found out, positive and lasting change is not easy. Once you've made a commitment to change, identified your goal and developed a few target behaviors, you are ready to move to the next phase of the change process. In this phase you need to prepare to change by getting ready to overcome the obstacles to your success.

You may encounter your own internal obstacles when you try to break old habits. You may also face resistance from others around you who don't want to see you change. If you're not prepared to deal with these challenges, you stand a good chance of caving in and returning to the very behavior that you want to change.

Rather than being taken by surprise, anticipate the problems that you may encounter and have plans to ensure that you will be successful in overcoming them. That's why good preparation is critical. Without it, your chances of success are far less. There are several techniques that are helpful in making final preparation for your successful change.

Step 11. Identify Obstacles Standing in Your Way

"The will to win is worthless if you don't have the will to prepare."

Thane Yost

Undoubtedly, you will face obstacles when you begin the process of changing your behavior. Some of these obstacles may revolve around your own insecurity in trying to act a different way. As you behave differently you may also run into critical or unsupportive comments from those around you. Anticipating the obstacles you may face is important so you can develop strategies to deal effectively with them in the event that they materialize. Here is an exercise that will help:

Exercise 11a: Identify obstacles to change
Take a page in your journal and divide it lengthwise into two columns. Title the first column on the left side of the page "Personal Obstacles" and the column on the right side of the page, "Environmental Obstacles". (Before we move forward, let me define a few terms. Personal obstacles are the limitations that you intentionally or unintentionally construct to defeat yourself such as self-consciousness, surrendering to your fears, lack of priorities, etc. Remember, your old behavior has been a comfortable way of dealing with your work-related circumstances. Don't assume that you will easily give up your old behavior patterns. Environmental obstacles, on the other hand, are those limitations that are superimposed on you by others or your organization.) Now, under each column list the obstacles that you feel will stand in the way of your success. All the defeating personal behaviors should be listed under the heading "Personal Obstacles" and all the potential limitations put in your way by others or your organization should be listed under the heading of "Environmental Obstacles. Then next to each obstacle you have listed assign a number based on a "1" to "3" scale. Let "1" represent an obstacle that is easy to overcome. Let "2" represent an obstacle that is more difficult

but you feel confident that you can overcome it with hard work. A level "3" indicates an obstacle that is truly insurmountable. If you have identified an obstacle as a level "3" think about it again. Are you sure that there isn't a way that you could overcome it? Will it really prohibit you from changing the unwanted and unproductive behavior that is stopping you from getting all you want from your job or career? Could you approach the obstacle in a new and creative way? In reality, very few of my clients assign a rating of "3" to any obstacle they face after they think it through. However, if it is truly insurmountable and you feel that you will fail in your change effort, then you are likely to be doomed to repeat your unwanted behavior until the obstacle is either diminished in its power or completely removed. If you feel that you can't overcome all obstacles then carefully consider how badly you want to change. If you are unsure of your commitment then review the material from Chapter 3 and see if you can't rekindle the energy around your positive change process.

Step 12. Develop Effective Coping Strategies
You have now identified the obstacles that could interfere with your success. However, simply knowing them is not enough; you need a way over, under, around or through them. Here is an exercise that helps many of my clients find effective coping strategies that will get them to their goal.

Exercise 12a: Develop your coping strategies
Review the exercise above in which you identified potential obstacles to your success. Pay particular attention to those obstacles that you have listed as a "2" since these will likely be more problematic to overcome. For each obstacle that you've listed, write a description of an effective coping strategy. To do this, consider how you may have successfully attempted a change in the past. What has previously worked to help you address a similar obstacle? Using proven coping strategies that have worked for you in the past is an excellent way to capitalize on solid techniques that have already demonstrated their worth. If you can't recall any previous

successful examples, then think creatively about how you might address the obstacle. Let me give you a few examples. As a personal strategy, if you think that you might be nervous and unsure about trying a new behavior, then one coping strategy is to talk positively to yourself just before you try out the new behavior. Positive self-talk is an excellent way to bolster your self-confidence. You might also discuss your concern with one or more of your peer coaches. Ask them to help you build up your sense of confidence. There are also some common coping strategies to tackle environmental obstacles. One strategy, for example, is to simply tell the people blocking your success that you are in the process of changing the way you previously dealt with them. Then let these individuals know what new behavior they can expect from you in the future. A second strategy is to try to identify and address their vested interest and show them how your new behavior might be of greater benefit to them (or at least, won't hurt or negatively impact them). Of course, these are only examples used for illustration purposes. The list that you create will be based on what works for you and should be your guide as you deal with these two categories of obstacles.

Step 13. Develop Your Action Plan

Action plans need to be developed for *each target behavior*. A good plan is a detailed series of action-oriented steps that will lead you to perform your target behavior. It should also include the timeframes in which you will complete each action step and the resources (people, training program, etc.) that you will need. An action plan helps you focus your energy and efforts on the target behavior, and makes your steps intentional and focused. It helps you think through what you are going to do, when it will be done, and what you'll need to accomplish it. Investing time now in creating a good action plan will save you time, effort and frustration in the longer run.

In developing your plan, it is important to take small and success-oriented steps that will build your confidence. As an example, let's assume for the moment that you are uncomfortable speaking before a group. You feel that your nervousness is holding you back in your career. Your coaching goal is to confidently deliver the speech in front of an audience.

One of your target behaviors is to reduce the level of nervousness that you feel in front of a group of people. Rather than set yourself up for failure by suppressing your anxiety and walking into a room full of people to make your presentation, you would be better served by taking a few more preparatory steps to reduce your nervousness. As the first step in your action plan, for example, you may practice a speech before a mirror 10 times by the end of the week with the goal of becoming assured of your ability to deliver the speech. Then as the second step you may give the speech within the next two weeks to a small group of close friends, a few colleagues or your spouse. The third step may be to actually deliver the speech in front of a large audience in the next month with the goal of giving the speech in a way that you felt confident and assured. The point is that small successes lay the foundation for larger accomplishments. This is what an action plan is designed to do: itemize a series of small and success-oriented steps that lead to your goal.

Exercise 13a: Create your plan of action

For each target behavior, divide a page in your journal into three equal columns. For the first column write the title "*What* I will do". In the second column write the title, "*When* I will do it by." In the last column write, "The *resources* I need." Then complete the first column by listing the *detailed action steps* that will lead you to accomplishing your target behavior. Remember to consider how you will overcome personal and environmental obstacles. Design your plan so that you take small incremental steps, particularly at first. You can become bolder as you go along and begin to master new behavior patterns. In the second column write the timeframes in which each action step will be completed. In the last column make a list of the people, materials, and other resources that you will need to tap into to assist in accomplishing each action step. If any parts of your action plan change, revise the plan in your journal so you will always have an accurate record of your plan for success. Hold yourself accountable to making your plan work. Share it with your mentor

"Yard by yard, life is hard; but inch my inch, it's a cinch"

Robert Schuller

and peer coaches. Take it seriously. It is your road map for successful change.

Step 14. See Yourself as a Success

You are about ready to officially launch your new target behaviors. However, before you take action, you would be well-served to spend a little time and psychologically prepare yourself. I am suggesting that you must *see* yourself as being successful before you start *acting* successfully.

Let me give you an example that might help. When Jack and I began working together I asked him to recall the previous blow up he had with his boss. Then, I asked him to visualize how he might have handled the situation in a more productive manner. Together Jack and I talked through a variety of potential scenarios (e.g., "If my boss did this, then I would do that", etc.). Eventually, Jack felt that he had developed a variety of responses that he could employ with confidence in the many different situations that he might face in dealing with his boss. I asked Jack to visualize himself as successfully demonstrating these various responses. I also asked him to record in his journal how he was feeling about himself in these visualized situations. These exercises helped reinforce Jack's desired behavior and further integrate it into his behavioral repertoire. Armed with these resources, Jack was able to successfully confront his boss and constructively resolve their misunderstanding. Like Jack, your chances of being successful will improve if you can see yourself acting successfully.

Exercise 14a: See yourself overcoming obstacles
Take a moment and review your list of coping strategies from exercise 12a. Then think about a likely scenario in which you might be called upon to cope with a personal or environmental obstacle as you first begin your journey towards change. Now visualize yourself in that situation as you see yourself successfully acting out your coping strategy. What would you do? How would you like to react? If they did this, what would you do? Then, after you visualize yourself successfully overcoming the obstacle, take a moment to appreciate your feelings of success. Make a note of what you have learned and how you feel in your journal. Repeat this process for each obstacle that you have identified in exercise 11a.

Notes

Notes

Notes

Notes

CHAPTER 6

PHASE 5 - *TAKING ACTION*

Margaret was a bright, articulate and somewhat head-strong CEO of a mid-sized telecommunications firm that had been acquired by a large publicly traded technology company. As part of the transaction, Margaret signed an employment contact with the new company and had taken a job as a vice president reporting to the COO. Accustomed to being the prime decision maker, Margaret now found herself three levels down from the CEO and surrounded by a peer group that was well-versed in the internal politics of her new company. Within the first few months of Margaret's employment she had several unfortunate and tense encounters with some of her peers over their lack of meeting timelines and reaching corporate goals. Since their poor performance impacted her responsibilities, she felt justified in demanding accountability. Before long, she found herself being treated as an outsider and often missed the informal peer to peer communications prevalent in her new company. When I initially met with Margaret she was frustrated, isolated and unable to get her job done. Together we went through the initial phases of change and crafted an action plan. However, as she began to implement the plan, she found herself stumbling.

This phase in the change process requires you to leave the safety of the boat, jump into the water and start swimming. As you will see, however, taking action to achieve your target behaviors is more than just being active and religiously following an action plan. There is a major difference between *mere activity* and *taking effective action*.

It is important to note that creating major changes in your behavior usually requires making significant accommodations to your regular behavioral routine. This involves restructuring certain parts of your activities on the job and the way you deal with others.

> *"The only thing that overcomes hard luck is hard work."*
>
> Harry Golden

There are a variety of common problems that you may encounter as you begin to take action. You may, for example, discover that you are not psychologically ready to change. You may find that your action plan may not be detailed enough to give you a good road map. If this is the case, you may easily veer off course. Another potential problem is that you may not be prepared for the hardship required to replace an old behavior with a new one. Additionally, you may be hoping for the "magic bullet" - the one single and simple solution that will bring lasting change. You may forget that successful change is a cumulative process that is built on a firm foundation of the steps contained in this workbook. You may believe that you can simply use your "willpower" to make a change. Let me warn you, willpower (by itself) is seldom sufficient to make a *lasting* change. As you begin to take action, however, there are some steps that will help ensure your success.

Step 15. Fine Tune Your New Behavior

When you first start demonstrating a new target behavior you may make one of two common errors. With the first type of error you are excited, energized and raring to go. As such, you may take too large of an initial step forward or push your new target behavior too far before you are sufficiently ready to effectively exhibit these new behaviors. You may appear to others like the proverbial "bull in a china shop". That is, your behavior is too exaggerated and you appear overly zealous. You need time to refine your new behavior so it becomes natural and produces the results you want. Rushing in with an untried major change in your behavior often only serves to alienate others and ultimately serves to reduce the level of confidence that you have in your ability to successfully change. The second common error has just the opposite effect. That is to say, you are so tentative and uncomfortable that you fail to take a sufficiently large step for people to notice a positive change in your behavior.

Both types of errors may lead to failure. In the first instance, it is because you will receive negative feedback from others who are overpowered by "the new you." In the second instance, it is because you never move far enough away from your old behavior so that you and others can actually see a perceptible change for the better. Below are a few exercises that will help you successfully modulate your new behavior so you don't make either mistake.

Exercise 15a: Check how others are responding
As you demonstrate your new target behavior, carefully observe how others are reacting. If people pull away or offer undue resistance, you are probably coming across too strong. However, if people seem to be treating you in the same old way and you are not noticing any kind of a reaction, you are probably coming across with little, if any, noticeable change in your behavior. It is also helpful to ask your peer coaches for feedback about how they see your new behavior. They can offer suggestions and insights that will be helpful. Take their thoughts and write them in your journal. Identify the specific actions that seem to be working and those that are not producing the desired results. Continue demonstrating and refining the behaviors that are effective.

Exercise 15b: Get in touch with how you are feeling
While input from others is extremely valuable, your personal feelings about how you are doing are also important. As you try out a new target behavior you should feel somewhat uncomfortable; after all it is a *new* behavior. It is expected (and desirable) that you will feel somewhat uncomfortable. In fact, if you are feeling totally comfortable in demonstrating your new behaviors you probably have not stretched yourself far enough. If this is the case, think of ways that you can be bolder in demonstrating your target behaviors. If you are feeling highly uncomfortable, however, you are probably taking things too fast and need to back off a bit. Remember, start with small incremental steps of modeling your new behavior and expand them once you are sure you are on the right track. Write in your journal what is

working and what isn't. Continue demonstrating and refining the behaviors that are working.

Exercise 15c: Rethink your new behavior
If you find your target behavior is not effective, the problem may lie in your action plan (you are taking on too much or too little) or in how you are conceptualizing (how you see yourself performing) your target behavior. You will need to determine which (or both) is causing the problem. Once you identify the problem you should make modifications to your action plan and/or how you envision yourself performing the target behavior.

Step 16. Continue to Anticipate Problems and Develop Alternate Strategies

It is important that you continue to anticipate the problems that you may encounter and design effective coping strategies to overcome the obstacles that you may face. Being forewarned is being forearmed. While you have previously attempted to identify the barriers you may face, chances are that you have not identified *all* of them. Most often, you will only find these other obstacles as you take action. Consequently, your plan needs to be continually updated with the new obstacles you anticipate and the appropriate coping strategies.

Exercise 16a: Anticipate future obstacles
Think about and make notes in your journal regarding any new obstacles that may interfere with your eventual success. Incorporate into your action plan these new personal and environmental obstacles by repeating exercise 12a. Then address new coping strategies as suggested in exercise 13a and 14a.

Step 17. Manage Temptations

Changing a long standing behavior does not happen overnight, nor does it happen without facing serious temptation to revert back to the old way of acting. After all, you have learned to rely on your previous behavior and now it has become an automatic response to a situation. Therefore, it is reasonable to assume that you will be tempted to fall back.

"Countering" is a proven change technique that works very well in the action stage to help overcome temptations to revert to the old behavior. The concept is easy. In countering, you simply substitute a new and positive behavior for your old and unwanted behavior. Interestingly, the way your mind works it is easier to stop one behavior by substituting another. For example, instead of continuing to eat throughout the evening (an unwanted behavior) you could substitute exercising (a positive and new behavior) after each meal. Each time you get the urge to eat at an unscheduled time, turn to exercise or substitute some other beneficial and rewarding activity in place of eating. In a similar manner, every time you want to fly off the handle at a co-worker, excuse yourself and take a short break to counter your unproductive behavior.

Many clients also find that you can counter an unwanted stress behavior (such as fear or tension) by substituting a relaxation response such a deep breathing. Studies have shown that just a few minutes of deep breathing produces a more positive state of mind. Deep breathing exercises release certain chemicals within your brain cells and improve blood circulation, both of which reduce your feelings of tension and anxiety.

Countering can also be useful for problems related to lack of self-esteem or poor self-confidence. Largely because of negative childhood experiences, you may lack the confidence that you can successfully change. Typically, your mind automatically plays negative messages when you are faced with a challenge. These internal "tapes" erode your feeling of confidence. You may tell yourself, for example, "I am stupid and I will fail." You literally "psych yourself out" by playing these negative messages over and over again (consciously and unconsciously.) This internal dialogue is commonly called "self-talk." Until you are able to program your own *affirming* thoughts, you will always be subject to negative messages that will defeat you. In other words, you need to counter your negative messages with positives ones. Here is an exercise that will help you overcome the temptation to fall back into your old behavior.

> *"Success is how high you bounce when you hit bottom."*
>
> George S. Patton

Exercise 17a: Counter temptations
Divide a page in your journal into two lengthwise columns. Label the column on the left "Temptations" and label the column in the right, "How I will counter temptations." Identify the temptations that you will face and list them down the page under the column labeled "Temptations." Now, think of one or more positive countering actions to help you overcome each temptation. Write these in your journal across from the appropriate temptation and in the column titled "How I will overcome temptations" Next, visualize yourself successfully substituting these positive action(s) as you face each temptation. Continue to practice these visualizations until you feel confident that you can successfully face and defeat each temptation. As you visualize, allow yourself to appreciate the good feelings that come from ridding yourself of the behaviors that you don't want and replacing them with positive ones. Continue to practice visualizations and allow yourself the feeling of accomplishment in defeating old behaviors. Write in your journal any insights you may have gained along with any comments about how you feel when you successfully counter an unwanted behavior. (You may want to revise your action plan to incorporate these new insights.)

Step 18. Avoid Provoking Situations

Remember the old saying, "If you don't want to drink, stay away from liquor"? It is pretty simple, yet effective advice. As a football coach once stated, "Good defense wins championships." As the action phase unfolds, some people purposely test themselves by seeking out negative stimuli. This is dangerous and you should avoid it like the plague. Rather than flirting with high risk situations that have the potential to set you back, spend your time thinking about how you will avoid or cope with them in a constructive manner.

Exercise 18a: Avoid negative stimuli
Review your previous list of negative antecedents from your journal (exercise 5a). As you'll remember, these antecedents stimulate the behavior that you want to change. Based on

what you now know about yourself, see if you can list any other negative antecedents. If so, write them in your journal. Next to each antecedent write one or two ways in which you will avoid it or cope with it. Now, visualize yourself acting out that positive coping response. By practicing this exercise, you will have an appropriate behavioral response already worked out in your mind when you are confronted with the real situation. You may want to update your action plan with this new information.

Step 19. Reward Yourself

Rewards, even small ones, are important in establishing and maintaining your new behavior. Make rewarding yourself a priority and be sure that you routinely recognize and appreciate the small successes along the way to your ultimate goal. Psychological studies have shown that giving rewards tends to establish a behavior while withholding rewards often will extinguish it. If you are not performing the old behavior, then you are not getting the reward you originally associated with it. Over time, this old behavior will go away because it is not being rewarded. Likewise, each time you reward yourself for performing your new and desired behavior, you are helping to establish it. So, on the one hand you are extinguishing the old and unwanted behavior (withholding the reward) while on the other hand you are establishing (giving the reward) the new and more desirable behavior. It's really a "win-win" situation. Sometimes rewards can simply be internal verbal messages in which you tell yourself that you have done "a good job." This is positive self-talk.

> *"There is only one difference between a good life and a good dinner: with the dinner the sweets come last."*
>
> Robert Louis Stevenson

Sometimes, external and tangible rewards (like a dinner out, getting new clothes, or seeing a favorite movie) can be intentionally structured to reinforce your successful behavior.

It is important to remember that lasting changes in your behavior will usually come through small and incremental steps. Unfortunately, many people fail in their early efforts to change because they expect too much too soon. Without building on a series of past success, they usually fail. It is wiser to seek smaller levels of solid improvement upon which you can build sustained and successful behavior over time.

Let me give you an example. Steve was a rather timid client who wanted to act more assertively at staff meetings, particularly when his boss was present. As an initial step, it would have been inadvisable for him to try to act assertively throughout the entire meeting. Rather, it seemed more prudent for him to set an initial objective of expressing an opinion on only one topic of discussion at the next staff meeting. After he had been successful in voicing his opinion, I instructed him to give himself a positive internal affirmation such as, "I expressed myself very well on that issue" or "Good job!" I also requested that he mentally recall his positive experience several times a day and continue to give himself a positive reinforcement each time. At the next staff meeting, he voiced his opinion on three issues and followed the same reinforcing procedure. Eventually, Steve was able to freely express his opinion on the issues that he felt were important. Building on incremental steps of successful behavior is laying a strong foundation for success.

Exercise 19a: Reward Yourself:
Write a list of rewards that you feel are meaningful and appropriate in your journal. After you have had a success (even a small one) in demonstrating a desired target behavior or taking a step in your action plan, pause a moment and reflect on your accomplishment and refer to the list. Give yourself a mental "pat on the back" or some other reward from the list that is meaningful to you. Then write in your journal how you are feeling about yourself when you successfully demonstrate a target behavior.

Step 20. Use Helping Relationships

During the action stage you are likely to encounter internal and external resistance to your efforts to change your behavior. Make no mistake, successful change takes perseverance and dedication in order to overcome temptations to revert to previous behavior patterns. Helping relationships focus you on the positive aspects of the change and provide encouragement for you to continue your efforts towards more effective behavior. Change does not happen alone, but with the help of others.

Exercise 20a: Use the "buddy system"

Call upon your mentor and a few of your most trusted peer coaches and develop a "support contract" with them. This will let them know what you expect. You must ask them to hold you accountable to do the things that will result in successfully reaching your goal. Explain that you are in the action stage and that you will need their help in a few important ways. For example, you might need their help in resisting the old negative antecedents (stimuli). If this is the case, tell your helpers that they can help you stay away from, or cope with, the situations that provoke your old unwanted behavior. You may also want some good old fashion moral support. That is, you need to be able to count on them to listen and offer encouragement. This will help you stay the course towards positive change. As you call upon them, record in your journal the positive encouragements they have offered and thoughts about your rekindled commitment to continue in your efforts to change. Remember to show your appreciation for those who have helped you.

"*Learning* is defined as a change in behavior. You haven't learned a thing until you take action and use it."

Don Shula

Notes

Notes

Notes

Notes

CHAPTER 7

PHASE 6 - *Maintaining Your Successful New Behavior*

Everything was working out fine for Sylvia. Once considered a distant and aloof supervisor, she had made great strides in improving communication with her staff. Her boss had even recommended Sylvia for promotion to Division Manager. She had followed her action plan to the letter. She was able to continue her new behavior for more than six months. Then, for reasons she couldn't put her finger on, Sylvia began to slip back into her old behavior. As she changed so did her staff. Once energized and motivated, her staff eventually became demoralized. Her boss even took notice of the poorer morale among Sylvia's direct reports. She became frustrated with her relapse but couldn't seem to muster the energy to break with her old habits. By the time Sylvia came to see me she considered herself as "hopeless." Was there anything she could do to help herself?

Silva mistakenly assumed that she was done with the change process once she had successfully changed her behavior for a brief period of time. On the contrary, studies have shown that attempts at change seldom fully succeed the first time. For example, the cigarette smokers who are very serious about quitting will attempt to stop smoking an average of four times before they are ultimately successful. Likewise, young adults who are ready to leave their parents home "permanently" return home again an average of three times before they are actually able to make the break for good. In fact, across a wide spectrum of people, researchers have found that only one in five are able to sustain the desired change on the first attempt. However, the good news is that you don't have to be haunted by the fear of eventual doom if you work hard to sustain your new behavior in the maintenance phase.

> *"Develop success from failures. Discouragement and failure are two of the surest stepping stones to success."*
>
> Dale Carnegie

Returning to your old behavior is called a "relapse." It has been estimated that in 60% to 70% of the cases of relapse, sudden stress (a job crisis, loss of a deep interpersonal relationship, etc.) is the culprit. However, other factors can also be involved. For example, sometimes people will become overconfident in their ability to sustain change and take their ability to demonstrate the new behavior for granted. They forget that success in changing behavior is defined by more than a few successful episodes of demonstrating a new behavior. In my experience as an executive coach, a relapse situation is frequently built on a series of small (even unconscious) acts in which clients gradually succumb to temptations and then revert to their old behavior. Once the regressive pattern begins, unsuspecting clients frequently find themselves on a "slippery slope" to relapse. That is why being especially vigilant during the maintenance phase is of such critical importance. Remember, in spite of your best efforts, relapse is common.

If you do slip, however, don't be discouraged. You need to refocus your energy and get back on the positive path towards change. Don't obsess over your failure. The simple truth is that maintaining a new behavior requires constant work. You must be willing to make change a high priority until your new behavior becomes automatic. Patience and persistence are keys to success in this phase.

Step 21. Keep Change a High Priority

You must keep your original commitment to change a high priority. Like Sylvia, it is easy to revert to your old and more comfortable way of behaving. Research indicates that people are more likely to maintain their new behavior if they keep the original reasons for their desired change fresh in their mind.

Exercise 21a:Review your pros and cons regularly
One way to keep change a high priority is to review from your journal the original list of pros and cons that gave rise to the desire for change (exercise 8a). Do this each time that you think you are apt to slip back into your old behavior. Add any new insights you might have and weight them using the five point scale as discussed in the exercise.

Exercise 21b: Reward yourself
Take time for reflection on all that you have accomplished. When you demonstrate your new behavior, give yourself a silent verbal reward or do something else nice for yourself. Review exercise 19a and pick a reward that is meaningful and appropriate. I also encourage my clients to continue their journaling even in this last phase. As you journal, be sure to write down the on-going successes you have had in changing your behavior and include some thoughts about how good being successful makes you feel. Remember, behavior is driven by rewards. Be sure you reward yourself sufficiently to reinforce the new and more positive behavior that you have worked so hard to master.

Step 22. Incorporate New Behavior into Your Self-Image
Whether you consciously realize it, as you've successfully completed these exercises you have gradually changed your self-image. You have learned to reject old troublesome behaviors and replace them with new and more effective ones. As you have done this, your level of confidence and your self-image have also improved. In order for your new self-image to become firmly established, however, you must keep appreciating that you are a more effective person than you once were.

Exercise 22a: Revitalize your self-image
Review exercises 6a, d and e. Remind yourself of the reasons why you did not like the old behavior and of the reasons that you wanted to develop your new behavior. Add any new insights to the list. If you feel you might slip, review the exercise as soon as possible and as often as needed to reinforce your new self-concept. Also write in your journal any positive feelings about your new self-image.

"Keep your mind off the things you don't want by keeping it on the things you do want."

W. Clement Stone

Step 23. Keep Countering

Continue substituting positive behavior for unwanted behavior. You should be focusing on strengthening the countering techniques that you learned in the preceding phase. Clients often report that they feel a nagging temptation to let down their guard and revert to the old behavior "just once." I often explain that this is like the devil inviting you into hell for a quick visit. There is no such thing. If you feel the temptation, you have not overcome your desire to resume your old and unwanted behavior. You must realize that temptations are real and, if they are left unchecked, they will draw you back into your old ways like a powerful magnet.

Exercise 23a: Continue to use countering techniques
Continue to practice the countering technique (exercise 17a). Add new positive countering behaviors where you feel they might help and write them in your journal. Continue to appreciate the progress you are making. Write down your positive feelings as you successfully see yourself overcoming your old behaviors.

Step 24. Use Helping Relationships

Helping relationships are also critical in this last phase of the change process. Make no mistake, the people who inspire you to continue your journey are your best allies as you drive towards sustained change. Because the exhilaration of the action stage is over, you may find that the commitment of your helpers has waned as you move into the maintenance stage. Therefore, you may need to re-enlist your peer coaches, and renegotiate their contract (or find new helpers). Below are two exercises that will help.

Exercise 24a: Get assistance from your peer coaches
Discuss with your peer coaches your ideal reaction to difficult situations where you may be tempted to revert to your old behavior. Have your peer coaches discuss with you how you might avoid the temptation to fall back into your

old ways. Consider their suggestions seriously, but remember that what works for them might not work for you. Select those strategies that you think will work and write them in your journal. Then visualize yourself being successful at demonstrating responses to these temptations. Write in your journal any new insights.

Exercise 24b: Help someone else become successful
Find someone else who wants to change an unwanted behavior and help him or her. See yourself as the "poster child" for positive change. The other person's problem doesn't have to be the same as yours. Share with them your knowledge and techniques regarding making a positive change in behavior. You will find yourself benefiting by helping someone else. When you articulate how you achieved your success you will find yourself being buoyed with more confidence and determination to stay the course. Take a moment and appreciate how far you have come to be able to help someone else embark on a change process which will improve his or her life. Write in your journal any new insights.

*D*iscipline is the bridge between goals and accomplishment."

Jim Rohn

Notes

Notes

Notes

Notes

CHAPTER 8

FINAL THOUGHTS

In addition to the information presented in this workbook, there are other factors that will also play an important role in your success.

1. *Practice, practice, practice*

You've heard, "Practice makes perfect." But do you know why? Learning new behaviors involves creating new connections in your brain. Each time you visualize yourself being successful or look at problems in a new way, you are expanding and changing the neurological connections in your brain. The more you repeat these exercises the stronger the new connections become. Eventually they replace the old pathways and become your dominant way of thinking and acting. Repetition of the exercises also moves the learning from your short term to long term memory and reinforces new neural pathways that help you change. Studies have shown that new memories are very unstable for the first hour after they are experienced. Therefore, visualization and feeling appreciation exercises, in particular, should be repeated several times within a 60 minute period to gain maximum advantage. Therefore, don't do the exercises just once. Practice them over and over.

2. *Take personal responsibility for your success*

One of the hallmarks of successful people is that they are willing to be responsible for their actions. To become successful in changing your unwanted behavior you need to take personal responsibility for the outcome. Take charge. Don't relegate yourself to being a passenger in your own life. Be willing to drive your future.

3. *Be healthy*

There is a great deal of research on the mind-body connection. As you embark on your journey towards a better life, adopt good health habits. For example:

- *Get sufficient sleep.* Sleep is important because it aids brain development. Psychological studies have shown that when people are deprived of a good night's sleep, their ability to integrate experiences and effectively use their cognitive (thinking) power is significantly reduced.

- *Watch your diet.* We are, after all, a physical being. Food is the only source of nutrients that feed the cells in our brain. What you eat can have a profound effect on your behavior. Your change process will require you to have physical as well as mental stamina. Eat a balanced diet.

- *Exercise regularly.* Physical exercise has many benefits, both physical and mental. Physically, exercise increases your metabolism, increases the strength of your heart, and expands your lung capacity. Mentally, exercise works by increasing a neurochemical that positively affects your mood. Integrate an exercise routine in your life to take maximum advantage of the "new you."

You Can Do It!

Remember, you can change your behavior to *SUCCEED @ WORK*! You can use this workbook to help you change almost any behavior that is holding you back from performing effectively. If you have conscientiously addressed each relevant step and completed the associated exercises, you are already well on the road to permanently changing your unwanted behavior. If you have failed in the past, it is probably because you were not sufficiently ready to change and you did not understand how to change. This workbook leads you through a step-by-step process to ensure that you are fully prepared to regain control over your job and career.

Notes

Notes

Notes

Notes

REFERENCES

Amen, Daniel, G., *Change Your Brain; Change Your Life* (1998), Three Rivers Press, New York.

Bandura, A., *Self-Efficacy: The Exercise of Control* (1997), W.H. Freeman & Company, New York.

Beck, A., and Emery, G., *Anxiety Disorders and Phobias* (1985), Basic books, New York.

Cloud, Henry, *Changes That Heal* (1992), Zondervan, Grand Rapids, MI.

Covey, Stephen, *The Seven Habits of Highly Effective People* (2003), Simon Schuster, New York.

Crabb, Larry, *Inside Out* (1988), NavPress, Colorado Springs, CO.

Conlan, Roberta (ed.), *States of Mind: New Discoveries about How Our Brains Make Us Who We Are* (1999), John Wiley & Sons, New York.

De Beauport, E., *The Three Faces of Mind: Think, Feel, and Act to Your Highest Potential* (2002), Quest Books, Wheaton, IL.

Gruman, A., and Messer, S., *Essential Psychotherapies: Theory and Practice* (1995), Guilford Press, New York.

Hedges, Burke, *Think & Grow Rich* (2000), INTI Publishing & Resource Books, Tampa, FL.

Helmstetter, S., *What to Say When You Talk to Yourself* (1982), Pocket Books, New York.

Kramlinger, K (ed.), *Mayo Clinic on Depression* (2001), The Mayo Foundation for Medical Education and Research, Rochester, MN.

Lodi, Kenneth, J., *Tapping Potential* (2000), The Catalyst Group, Los Angeles.

Maxwell, John, *Thinking For a Change* (2003), Warner Books, New York.

Miller, R., and Mason, S., *Diagnosis Schizophrenia: A Comprehensive Resource* (2002), Columbia University Press, New York.

Prochaska, J, Norcross, J, and DiClemente, C., *Changing For Good: A Revolutionary Six Stage Program For Overcoming Bad Habits And Moving Your Life Positively Forward* (1994), Harper Collins Publishers, New York.

Quinn, Robert, E., *Deep Change* (1996), Jossey-Bass, San Francisco.

Quick Order Form

Please send me _____ copies of *Succeed @ Work*. Payment must be enclosed.

Order Information:
Name:_____
Mailing address:_____
_____

Phone number: ( ) _____ Email: _____

Shipping information (if different from above):
Ship to: _____
Shipping address: _____
_____

Order:
_____ copies of *Succeed @* Work @ $19 ea $ _____

Shipping and handling (no charge)

Total $ _____

Payment:
__ check   __ credit card:
                        __ AMEX   __ MasterCard
                        __ Visa   __ other (specify)
Card number:_____
Name on card: _____
Signature: _____Exp date: _____

Fax a copy of this form to: (805) 492-4412.
Telephone orders: Call (805) 492-3400. Have your credit card ready.
Email orders: Orders@FastBreakPress.com
Postal orders: FastBreak Press, Order Department, P.O. Box 7382,
        Thousand Oaks, CA 91359-7382.